This Journal Belongs to

_____

Date

_____

"Jen Norton's *Arise to Blessedness* blends the artist's clear and powerful drawing with rich textures and nuanced colors—a wonderful way to explore depths of meaning in the Beatitudes through art. Norton points out that Jesus speaks to his followers 'in ways they know, affirming their dignity,' and her *Via Pulchritudinis* ('Way of Beauty') does exactly that, illustrating the loveliness of virtue and its many manifestations across places, traditions, and cultures."

Elizabeth Lev
Vatican art historian and author of
How Catholic Art Saved the Faith

"*Arise to Blessedness* is a creative masterpiece. Each saint is an accomplished guide; each image, a well-spring of contemplation; and each chapter, an opportunity to delve ever deeper into what it means to be truly blessed."

Allison Gingras
Author of *Encountering Signs of Faith*

"With beautiful artwork, insightful reflections, and stories told in a way to remind us that saints are more like us than not, this journal offers a means of honest reflection that will certainly allow you to go deeper in your journey to the heart of Jesus."

Marcia Lane-McGee
Cohost of *Plaid Skirts and Basic Black* podcast

A Journal Retreat with Eight
Modern Saints Who Lived the Beatitudes

Arise to Blessedness

Jen Norton

AVE MARIA PRESS AVE Notre Dame, Indiana

Founded in 1865, Ave Maria Press is a ministry of the United States Province of Holy Cross.

www.avemariapress.com

Paperback: ISBN-13 978-1-64680-186-2

E-book: ISBN-13 978-1-64680-187-9

Cover and interior artwork © Jen Norton.

Cover and text design by Katherine Robinson.

Printed and bound in the United States of America.

Library of Congress Cataloging-in-Publication Data is available.

This book is dedicated to all the brave souls
who serve their neighbor without regard
for honor and who love the unlovable
because they see Christ in everyone.

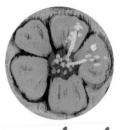

Contents

Preface: Prepare the Way   viii

How to Use This Journal   xii

1: Blessed Are the Poor in Spirit—St. André Bessette   1

2: Blessed Are They Who Mourn—St. Elizabeth Ann Seton   17

3: Blessed Are the Meek—St. Maximilian Kolbe   33

4: Blessed Are They Who Hunger and
Thirst for Righteousness—St. Mark Ji Tianxiang   49

5: Blessed Are the Merciful—St. Maria Goretti   65

6: Blessed Are the Clean of Heart—St. Charbel Makhlouf   81

7: Blessed Are the Peacemakers—St. Óscar Romero   97

8: Blessed Are They Who Are Persecuted—
St. José Luis Sánchez del Río   113

Conclusion: Rejoice and Be Glad, for Your
Reward Will Be Great   127

Acknowledgments   136

Arise to Blessedness Journaling Pages   138

PREFACE: *Prepare the Way*

The longest journey you'll ever make is the journey from the head to the heart.

—*Lissa Rankin*

When he [Jesus] saw the crowds, he went up the mountain, and after he had sat down, his disciples came to him.

—*Matthew 5:1*

A few years ago, my husband and I were invited to climb Croagh Patrick, a holy mountain in County Mayo, Ireland, where St. Patrick is said to have fasted for forty days. The 2,500-foot (764 m) climb is a popular Irish pilgrimage. People of all levels of ability from every country of the world attempt to reach its summit 365 days of the year, no matter the weather. Some barely make it, some run to the top, and some hobble up barefoot as a penitential practice.

Punctuated by beautiful green pastures of grazing sheep, rock formations, and rivers, the last third of the climb is a strenuous navigation over loose, slippery quartzite at a forty-five-degree angle. Encompassing both beauty and struggle, the mountain offers an accurate metaphor for pondering the Beatitudes from Jesus's Sermon on the Mount (see Mt 5:1–12).

Just before the toughest part of the climb, hikers reach a plateau where they can rest and reconsider whether continuing is worth the trouble. Many turn away and head back down, too weary to go any farther. My husband and I intended to get to the top, so after a brief rest, we carried on. It is during this last section of the climb that inexperienced hikers like myself must walk by faith, one step at a time—painfully aware that as the narrow path twists and turns, our feet may slip out from under us as we climb that steep peak.

On the day we hiked, the fog was thick and there was no way to visualize the final destination. What kept us going were all the hikers heading back down and encouraging us along the way. "It's just a few more turns," they'd say. "You're nearly there!" Their optimism was more kind than true, but we had already come so far. We couldn't turn back now!

At long last, when we finally reached the summit, we were rewarded with a small chapel, a donation box, and (miracle of miracles) a bathroom with running water. Heaven! But the real sense of accomplishment was the fulfillment of the journey shared with everyone who had made it all the way. There was a spirit of common awe with others at the top, a sense that we were part of a chosen few who embraced the whole challenge as something worthy. As we ate our sack lunches and congratulated ourselves on a job well done, we relished the joy in having reached our goal. We were thankful we didn't give up. On that day, we felt blessed.

In Jesus's Sermon on the Mount, he lays out his way to eternal happiness, or "blessedness." It is a countercultural call, often asking us to embrace what the rest of the world shuns. At the end of Matthew 4, Jesus invites Simon Peter, James, and John to follow him. As I read this passage, I hear Jesus extend an invitation to each of us—regardless of the circumstances of our lives—to come follow him as well.

Notice that in his sermon Jesus does not broadcast the principles of his kingdom all at once to the crowds following him. Rather, he goes up the mountain, sits down, and waits for the disciples to follow. Not the whole crowd—just the disciples—those who already know him and want to hear more.

Clearly, not everyone is ready for a countercultural change of heart. Jesus offers truth, goodness, and beauty, but he waits for our hearts to desire them. He waits while we hang out among the crowds, trying every other logical human attempt at happiness first. He waits while we confront the falsehoods of absolute security and "us versus them." He waits until we let go of control and judgment. He waits, in love, for you and me.

Jesus doesn't babble on to his followers with overly educated rhetoric. He teaches from the heart, using simple words that common working men and brokenhearted women understand. He speaks to them in the ways they know, affirming their dignity. He backs up his ideas with parables to ponder. And he leaves them with a simple prayer, the Our Father, to reinforce his words. "Lay down your fears and follow me," he says. "Your reward in heaven will be great."

It sounds easy. But like climbing a mountain, living the Beatitudes is hard. There is no funicular or helicopter to whisk us easily to spiritual bliss. The path is often irregular, unkept, and circular, causing us to rewalk the same experiences again and again with only a slight change in elevation. We can't see the end we hope for, and sometimes we must walk too close to the edge for comfort. We are asked only to keep trying, to keep looking up.

As we set off in the early morning on the day of our mountain hike, I found myself experiencing some trepidation about the adventure ahead. *It's going to be hard. It might rain. Why did I agree to do this? I could have just stayed comfortably in bed!* Underlying all of that was fear. Fear that I wouldn't be up to the climb. Fear that I'd bumble along and be a disappointment to my companions. Fear of pain and suffering. Fear that I wouldn't be good enough.

The father of lies likes to get into our heads like that, telling us with each new desired venture that we are not worthy. "Better to stay safely in place and preserve your energy," he whispers. "Let someone else do the hard work. You don't want to look like a fool, do you?"

And yet, to not even try was a worse option. If I let the opportunity to climb that mountain pass by, I would certainly never know the view from the top. To turn back and forfeit the spiritual gifts granted by the more arduous journey would have been the bigger disappointment. On this day, I had what I needed for the trip: decent health and fitness, a walking stick, and good boots. I had a bit of food and a desire to succeed. And I had friends I trusted who knew the way. Even if I didn't reach the peak, I could not allow my fear to stop me from trying.

My prayer for you is that, in reading this book, you will be inspired to climb the mountains of your life as well.

How to Use This Journal

In this book, we will meet eight saints from the modern era who chose to trust God beyond their own understanding. Like the original twelve disciples, once they knew Jesus first-hand, they could not unknow him and followed after him the rest of their lives, climbing that mountain all the way to heaven. Consequently, their lives illuminate the virtues of the Beatitudes.

Because these eight men and women are friends of Jesus, they are friends we can trust. Each saint can encourage us forward as we reflect on our own progress and discover what we are truly made of and for.

Each chapter follows a similar format:

- An original illustration with the chapter's key verse (Beatitude).

- A brief scripture reading, including a designed verse and a slightly longer reading related to the Beatitude.

- An image of the saint along with a brief introduction and "Warm Up" prompt, followed by a reflection on that saint.

- A guided "Visio Moment." Visio divina is a traditional prayer practice, similar to lectio divina, guiding you to a deeper encounter with God through sacred art.

- A "Journal Challenge" and "Today's Small Step" to prepare you to delve more deeply into what you have discovered.

- "This Is My Story" provides ample space for you to create, write, draw, and express your response to the

Beatitude or the saint's story as it pertains to your life. Do you have hopes, fears, or ideas about living that Beatitude more fully? Let your imagination lead you to ponder each of Jesus's promises in light of your own blessings, trials, and story.

Each of these journal prompts and prayer exercises are intended to help you engage the text and artwork in a more personal way. You can write directly in the journal if you choose (you will find ample writing space throughout the book), or you might decide to record your thoughts in a dedicated notebook. Feel free to unleash your own creativity in recording your responses. Drawing, writing, sketching, singing, and other artistic expressions are all good ways to process and express your reflections along the journey.

Here are three ways this journal can help you to get the most out of your personal journal retreat—and befriend these saints of the Beatitudes!

- *Take time to sit with Jesus.* Jesus invites each of us up to his ultimate wedding feast of heaven and earth. He promises us a life where what we have learned and practiced in the physical realm is joined with his Divine Love in the eternal realm.

  As we will see in the lives of these saints, the way of the Beatitudes readies us to full communion with Jesus and helps us become our most fully conscious selves, unhindered by fear or darkness. Where you find fear, let the saints' stories, Bible verses, journal prompts, and prayers take you deeper into trust.

- *Ponder the story as it relates to your life.* Saints are in many ways just like us; during their lifetimes, they had to overcome many of the same weaknesses and faults that we face every day. And yet they reached their reward by staying close to Jesus and choosing to persevere.

In researching the lives of these holy men and women, I listened for the ways they walked toward Jesus within their life circumstances, asking myself, "Would I do the same?" In some cases, I knew I would: I had faced and survived the particular challenges those saints had endured. But in other cases, I wasn't so sure—I still had fears to overcome, rough edges in need of refinement.

And so, I turn to the saints for guidance, knowing that they can pray for me with real insight, having a more complete perspective of their stories (as well as my own). Just like the hikers coming back down Croagh Patrick on our pilgrimage, they chant their encouragement to us as we make our own way up the path: "You're nearly there—it's just around the bend!"

- *"Read" and respond to the artwork.* As you reflect on each Beatitude in this book, take time to notice how it is portrayed in the artwork, giving it time to sink in. Allow this process of discovery to unleash your own creative expression in response.

    For example, the "mountain" metaphor appears in each piece in relation to the figure. It might be dark and enclosing as in "Blessed are they who mourn," or joyfully surmounted as in "Blessed are the pure of heart." *Where are the mountains in your life that God is calling you to climb?*

    There is always a source of light, but it might seem bright and near or dim and far. Is the light reaching down to the soul, or is the soul striving for the light? *What sources of light are you experiencing right now?*

Notice the small details. Birds indicate movement of the Holy Spirit, rocks and boulders imply difficulties, and the colorful lines of light that wind through each piece illustrate the force of a God who is closer to us than our very breath, permeating all life. Let the artwork in this book help you consider your own story and how you both seek and resist living the Beatitudes.

Writing this book has allowed me to look more closely at my own heart in light of the Beatitudes, and my prayer for you is that you will let the experience of this self-guided retreat travel with you and deepen your own understanding as well. My hope is that someday you will be able to sit with Jesus at the top of the mountain, feel the warmth of his healing touch, and know that it was all for you.

Blessed Are the Poor in Spirit

ST. ANDRÉ BESSETTE

My grace is Sufficient for YOU, FOR POWER is madePerfect in Weakness.

2 COR 12:9

A Scripture Reading

As he passed by he saw a man blind from birth. His disciples asked him, "Rabbi, who sinned, this man or his parents, that he was born blind?" Jesus answered, "Neither he nor his parents sinned; it is so that the works of God might be made visible through him."

—John 9:1–3

SAINT
ANDRÉ
Bessette

*"Blessed are the poor in spirit,
for theirs is the Kingdom of heaven."*

St. André Bessette of Montreal
(Alfred Bessette)

Born August 9, 1845, in Québec, Canada.
Died January 6, 1937, age ninety-one.

Beatified May 23, 1982.
Canonized October 17, 2010.

Feast Day: January 6 (January 7 in Canada)

Patron saint of home caregivers.

Warm Up: How does this image speak to you?

One Small Step

ST. ANDRÉ BESSETTE

Welcoming humility can be scary. If you excel at a particular skill, you might take pride in being defined primarily by your ability. But God is the source of every gift. Our aptitudes, big and small, are merely tools by which he might lead us into deeper being.

When we lose sight of this, pride can wreak havoc in our lives. Believing we are in control, we feel anxious as we compare ourselves to others. Attempting to maintain composure, we are driven to find fault in others and defend our egos. Fearful hearts harden with walls of arrogance, keeping peace and love at arm's length. But that's no way to reach the promise of eternal happiness. No, for this journey into living the Beatitudes, we must embrace our poverty of spirit.

Those who are "poor in spirit" are open to receiving God's grace precisely because they know how much they need it. St. André Bessette, the "Miracle Man of Montreal," reminds us that God loves even the most fragile among us.

Brother André wasn't considered valuable by worldly standards—his greatest spiritual assets were hidden within his "inability." Born poor and sickly, he lost both his parents while he was young. He could not read until age twenty-five, yet God held a vision for his life. Because of his prayerful devotion to St. Joseph, as a young man he desired to join the Congregation of Holy Cross, an order dedicated to his patron saint, but worried that he wasn't smart enough to fit in with its highly educated members. Likewise, the religious resisted accepting someone so prone to illness.

André turned to prayer, asking for St. Joseph's intercession. His prayer was answered, and he was accepted as a lay brother and given the unassuming job of doorman at the Collège Notre-Dame in Côte-des-Neiges in Montréal. For the next forty years he happily welcomed all visitors, wanting only to "serve God in the most obscure tasks."

But wait, there is more: God promoted him from the doorstep to the spotlight by giving the chronically ill man the gift of healing! He became the catalyst of hundreds of healing miracles among the students and community members, even curing an infant's brain tumor after he caressed the child's head. So many people came to seek his healing touch that he had to hire secretaries and receive the sick off-site. Through it all, he refused credit for any of the healings, insisting only that St. Joseph was working through him. He remained obedient to his calling, and when skeptics pressured the bishop to stop the healings, St. André replied that "he would obey blindly." The bishop instructed, "Then let him alone. If this work is from God, it will live; if not, it will crumble away."

The miracles continued and St. André's prayers to St. Joseph led to the building of the St. Joseph's Oratory of Mount Royal, where he served as the shrine's guardian until his death in 1937. St. André shows us not only how God works through us when we set aside pride, but how he actually needs us to embrace our poverty to hear his will. When we are poor in spirit, we become conduits for his love in action. We can become healers of souls for the kingdom of heaven.

Write your Thoughts:

Prepare to Climb

A VISIO MOMENT

Turn again to the beginning of this chapter, to the image of the mountain. At the bottom, you will find an image of a man emerging from the darkness with a wolf barking at his heels. He is only looking forward, mindful of his next step. He cannot see that heaven is at the end of his journey, at the top of the mountain, which is far from him. He is not concerned with looking up, only with looking forward to where he is being led by the Spirit, doing his best not to stumble on the rocks and roots.

Where do you see yourself in this picture? Where have you found stumbling blocks or moments of encouragement in your own journey?

JOURNAL ✒ CHALLENGE

St. André Bessette said, "Those who are cured quickly often are people who have no faith or little faith. On the other hand, those who have solid faith are not cured so quickly, for the good God prefers to allow them to suffer so that they will be sanctified even more."

What do you think of this statement? Does it affect the way you see those who struggle? How do you view this statement in light of your own suffering? Do you view hardships as punishment or a gift?

True humility is present even when no one is looking. When was the last time you felt God working in you and through your talents to show his love to the world? Did others recognize your efforts, and how did that make you feel? Write a prayer, inviting God into your reflection. Ask him to show you his plan.

TODAY'S SMALL STEP

St. André maintained a lifelong devotion to St. Joseph, asking for his intercession in his most humble moments and crediting the saint with his achievements. Find a saint, a scripture passage, or an affirmation that you can turn to for guidance this week as you encounter opportunities to be humble. Does having this reference change or add awareness to your actions? Write about your experiences.

This Is My Story

ARISE TO BLESSEDNESS

ARISE TO BLESSEDNESS

My Prayer Today

Our Father, who art in heaven, hallowed be thy name.

Dear Jesus:

Help me grow in humility and embrace my poverty so that I may always look up to you, not down on your creation. Come into my littleness and heal me. Fill the empty spaces in my soul with your awesome power. Help me to follow your holy will, even when I cannot fully comprehend it. Teach me, like St. Joseph, to adore Jesus and make him the center of my world. St. André Bessette, pray for me. *Amen.*

Blessed Are They Who Mourn

ST. ELIZABETH ANN SETON

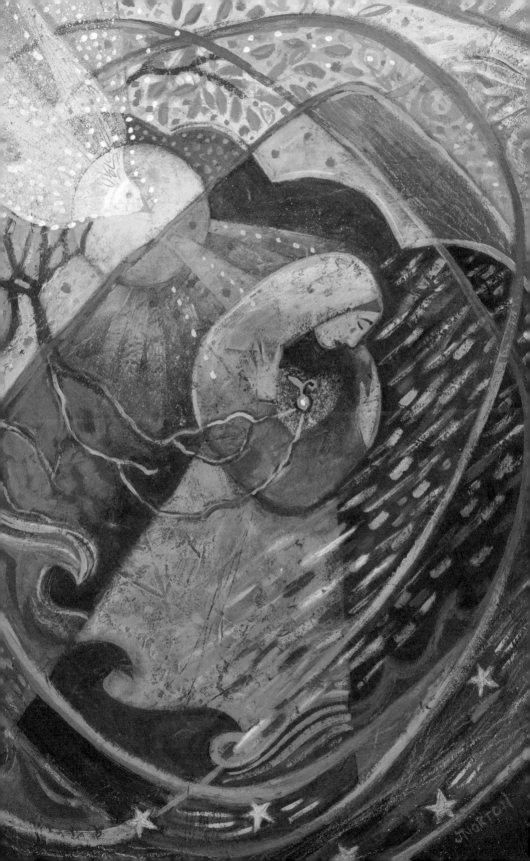

Because He himself was tested through what he suffered He is able to help those who are being tested.

Hebrews 2:18

A Scripture Reading

You will weep and mourn, while the world rejoices; you will grieve, but your grief will become joy. . . . I will see you again, and your hearts will rejoice, and no one will take your joy away from you.

—John 16:20, 22

St. Elizabeth Seton

"Blessed are they who mourn, for they shall be comforted."

St. Elizabeth Ann Seton

Born August 28, 1774, in New York City.
Died January 4, 1821, age forty-six.

Beatified March 17, 1963.
Canonized September 14, 1975.

Feast Day: January 4

Patron saint of seafarers, teachers, schools (including Catholic schools), in-laws, widows, those bereaved of parents and children. First American to be canonized.

Warm Up: How does this image speak to you?

Seeds of Life

ST. ELIZABETH ANN SETON

Unexpected loss is a heavy cross to bear. We breathe out in leaden sobs, mourning what was and what could have been, holding our breath in fearful anticipation of what might come next. But God always sees what could be, both here on earth and in heaven. He uses both loving and losing to refine us for eternal life. When we cry, "Why me?" he answers our plea with, "So you might come closer to my Sacred Heart and know who you really are. Just breathe."

St. Elizabeth Ann Seton was known for her kindness, charity, and witty humor—which is amazing, given the great losses she suffered. A succession of losses and recoveries had imprinted her soul with God's faithfulness in all things. Her childhood wealth and privilege were tempered with the early loss of her mother and the subsequent estrangement with her beloved stepmother soon after her separation from Elizabeth's father.

Elizabeth married into a prominent shipping family with a heart for charity and every promise of a comfortable life, but more loss ensued. With the death of her father-in-law and political strife in the newly forming American nation, family fortunes dissolved. Shortly after moving their family to Italy to improve her husband's health, Elizabeth's husband died and she found herself widowed far from home, a necessary recipient of the very charity to "poor widows with small children" that she had helped foster in New York. One can imagine the temptation to despair might have been great. Elizabeth had it all—and seemingly lost it all.

If we let it, loss and desolation can clarify truth and goodness as we let go of past obligations and emotional crutches and wholeheartedly seek God's consolation. In those moments, we often find God close at hand. So it was for Elizabeth, who was introduced to the Catholic faith by the family of her husband's Italian business partner. She found comfort from her losses in the promise of the Eucharist: for in partaking of the physical Body of Christ, we become part of a larger, mystical story. Remembering Jesus's own words in Gethsemane, "Thy will be done," helped her reframe her own suffering and consider new purpose.

Returning to America, she started an academy for young ladies, but anti-Catholic sentiment threatened her only source of income. A visiting Sulpician priest who had fled persecution under France's Reign of Terror offered her a chance to found a Catholic girls school. It would become the beginning of the parochial school system in America. She went on to found a religious community to help the poor children called the Sisters of Charity of St. Joseph (now Daughters of Charity).

St. Elizabeth Ann Seton could have turned bitter and lonely after losing everything that had seemed to define her. Instead, she found solid ground in God and a rekindled love for service. The seeds of charity planted in her youth, mellowed with compassion for those who suffer loss, produced a legacy of Catholic education and religious community that lives far beyond her short life of only forty-six years. She came to understand that we don't deserve anything, but God is always working to give us everything. We can learn from St. Elizabeth Ann Seton how to let go and trust God to shape our lives in this temporary world, preparing us for what he promises in heaven. Our mourning has purpose. We will breathe in again.

Write your Thoughts:

Prepare to Climb

A VISIO MOMENT

Turn again to the mountain image on page seventeen, and reflect a moment on what you see. When we mourn, we turn inward and, at least for a time, are unable to see or feel goodness and light. In this painting, the figure leans into the darkness, holding herself together. She cannot yet see that the light is just behind her, waiting for her to turn and recognize it. Her stars have fallen, waves threaten to undermine her footsteps, and rain pummels her. But within her broken heart is a seed, planted and starting to sprout roots. God's Spirit surrounds her in the natural world and is rushing toward her.

Have you ever felt such deep desolation? What are some practices you can put in place to protect yourself from despair in hard times?

JOURNAL ✒ CHALLENGE

Ask yourself, "If I lose everything that defines me, who am I? Who does God say I am?" If you have been through a time of loss, reflect on the gifts that eventually emerged from that difficult time. If not, write about your fears and your difficulties in trusting God for what might be in store for you.

Do you cling to your past or rely on old coping mechanisms from childhood, even though they do not serve your spiritual growth now? How might you let go of burdens that keep you fearful? How might you allow Jesus to transform your sadness into a joy?

Our God showed his vulnerability through suffering so he could walk with us in ours. St. Elizabeth Ann Seton said, "How sweet the [Eucharistic] presence of Jesus to the longing, harassed soul! It is instant peace, and a balm to every wound." As you receive Communion, gaze upon the crucifix and ponder the extent to which God has gone in order to be with you for eternity in both body and soul. Do you trust that all things, even hard things, have eternal purpose? Are you willing to trust God with everything you are?

TODAY'S SMALL STEP

Make a list of things you are afraid to lose. In another column, imagine how you might seek consolation after the loss of those things. Try to name each loss and find a corresponding action of consolation. (For example, the loss of a loved one to cancer might prompt you to make crocheted caps for cancer patients.)

This Is My Story

My Prayer Today

Thy kingdom come.

Dear Jesus:

When my plans fall apart and I am tempted to despair or turn to worldly comforts or addictions, help me remember that you have walked this road before me and shown me that there is life ahead. Speak to me in my loss and tell me who I am. Help me let go of my plans and expectations and embrace what comes with compassion. Heal my broken heart. Please help. For as long as you let me live, let me live with purpose. St. Elizabeth Ann Seton, pray for me. *Amen.*

Blessed Are the Meek

ST. MAXIMILIAN KOLBE

Do to Others whatever You would have them do to You. This is the Law & the Prophets.

Matthew 7:12

A Scripture Reading

No one has greater love than this, to lay down one's life for one's friends. You are my friends if you do what I command you.

—John 15:13–14

"Blessed are the meek, for they will inherit the land."

St. Maximilian Kolbe

Born January 8, 1894, in Zdunska, Poland.
Died August 14, 1941, age forty-seven.

Beatified October 17, 1971.
Canonized October 10, 1982.

Feast Day: August 14

Patron saint of families, drug addiction recovery, prisoners, journalists, the pro-life movement.

Warm Up: *How does this image speak to you?*

Traveling Companions

ST. MAXIMILIAN KOLBE

Looking at photos of a young Maximilian Kolbe, it's easy to imagine him as a man of intense religious passions and political convictions. Whereas others living in wartime have become obsessive or violent, Kolbe was driven by his love of the Blessed Mother. His desire for the gentle, merciful love of Our Lady called him to the service of her Son. He chose to use his gifts to empower others to turn from sin to sainthood, rather than unleash his own political zeal. He knew how to lead, and he knew whom he was following.

While a humble soul is open to heaven's inspiration and a mournful heart is primed for compassion, a meek person consciously chooses the well-being of the other over his own desire for power, manipulation, or control. A meek soul is gentle and has mastery over his or her own thoughts and actions, never seeking to dominate or harm others. Meekness is not weakness, but rather the character to reframe hardships as opportunities to embody Christ's mercy. The meek look out for others and affirm life.

As a rambunctious young teen, Maximilian once asked the Blessed Mother what would become of him. In a vision, Our Lady responded by showing him two crowns: one red for martyrdom, the other white for purity. When asked to choose which he preferred, he opted for both. This vision cultivated his desire for sainthood, and he sought out opportunities to serve with the Conventual Franciscans. He also joined the military to defend Poland from Russian forces, under the patronage of Mary.

When he founded the Knights of the Immaculata to educate and encourage total consecration to the Blessed Virgin Mary, his work caught the attention of the Gestapo and he was arrested and imprisoned in Auschwitz. It was there that his life and passion culminated in a final act of meekness that led to the fulfillment of his childhood vision and his recognition as a saint.

When several prisoners were to be executed by starvation in reparation for an escaped inmate, St. Maximilian Kolbe volunteered to take the place of one condemned man who had a family. Kolbe survived for two weeks in an underground cell where he never ceased praying. The guards finally killed him with an injection of carbolic acid, unaware that their inhumane action to end his life would lead to his inheritance of that very land as the "Saint of Auschwitz."

St. Maximilian Kolbe's selfless act, which changed another man's fate, shows us that God is present in our pain and suffering. With meekness, we allow God to transform the ugliest of power and terror into beauty and goodness. When we are meek, we fight life's battles with love as our weapon, knowing it has already won.

Write your Thoughts:

ARISE TO BLESSEDNESS

Prepare to Climb

A VISIO MOMENT

Turn back to page thirty-three and look at the image of the mountain. In this painting, the lower part of the figure represents the culture, the world, and its dangers. A nest has fallen, and a snake is searching for its contents to devour. But the man is not helping the snake, nor is he walking by without noticing the nest. He is on his knees and has gently lifted the bird up, beyond the darkness, beyond the mountaintop, to the light. There he can sing and be part of the flow of life where he belongs.

Where are the places in your life that you are called to look out for the interests of others?

JOURNAL / CHALLENGE

What are the triggers in your life that cause you to protect your status or dignity instead of offering yourself in service of God? Ponder your feelings and how you could become more aware of those provocations. Write a poem or prayer or draw a picture about how you could let go of your fears.

St. Maximilian Kolbe challenges us to consider if there is ever a reason to overpower another, even in the face of death. Think of a conflict you were engaged in, either with another person or with yourself in an internal battle. Do you see yourself as part of the solution or part of the problem? How can you change your thoughts or behavior for a different outcome?

St. Maximilian Kolbe saw his sacrifice for the other prisoner as fulfillment of his eternal purpose of becoming a saint. Have you ever held back from helping someone in need? Or have you stepped forward from your comfort zone to help? Ponder and write about your emotional responses to either situation. Did you feel God's presence in those times? Why or why not?

TODAY'S SMALL STEP

St. Maximilian Kolbe said, "He who loves the Immaculate will gain a sure victory in the interior combat." What battles do you fight interiorly that only you and God can see? Invite Mary into your heart and ask her to guide you by praying a daily Rosary for nine days (or by consecrating yourself to her Immaculate Heart).

This Is My Story

ARISE TO BLESSEDNESS

My Prayer Today

Thy will be done on earth as it is in heaven.

Dear Jesus:

When you ask me to be a channel of your peace, help me put aside my own sword in favor of your shield of loving-kindness. Teach me to see you in everyone, and let me be strong enough to kneel before you, next to Mary at the foot of the Cross, where you transform all things for your good. Let me have ears to hear your voice above all others. Give me courage to be an instrument of your mercy, not a hindrance. St. Maximilian Kolbe, pray for me. *Amen.*

Blessed Are They Who Hunger and Thirst for Righteousness

ST. MARK JI TIANXIANG

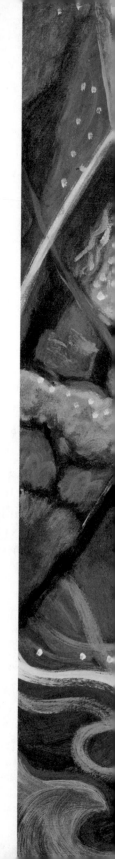

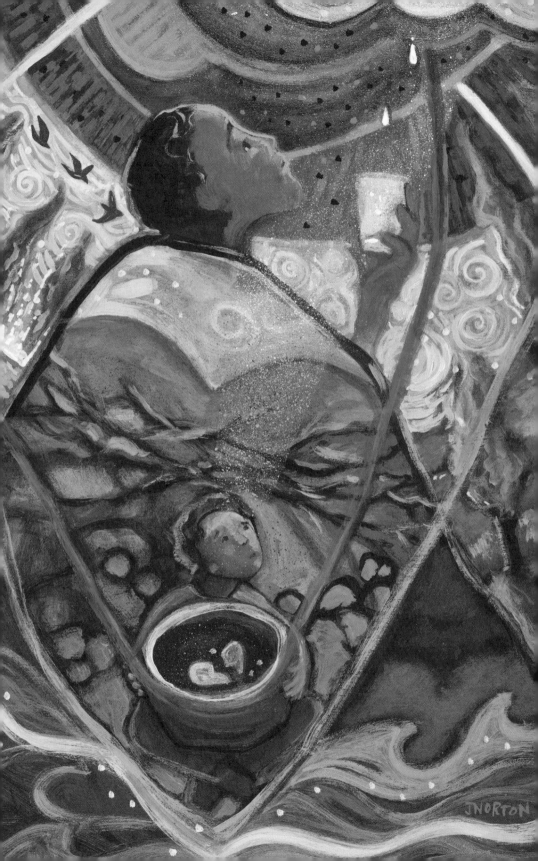

The Centurion said in reply, "Lord, I am not worthy to have you enter under my roof, only say the word & my servant will be healed."

Matthew 9:13

A Scripture Reading

I am speaking in human terms because of the weakness of your nature. For just as you presented the parts of your bodies as slaves to impurity and to lawlessness for lawlessness, so now present them as slaves to righteousness for sanctification. For when you were slaves of sin, you were free from righteousness. But what profit did you get then from the things of which you are now ashamed? For the end of those things is death. But now that you have been freed from sin and have become slaves of God, the benefit that you have leads to sanctification, and its end is eternal life. For the wages of sin is death, but the gift of God is eternal life in Christ Jesus our Lord.

—Romans 6:19–23

"Blessed are they who hunger and thirst for righteousness, for they will be satisfied."

St. Mark Ji Tianxiang

Born in 1834 in Hebei, China.
Died July 7, 1900, age sixty-five.

Beatified November 24, 1946.
Canonized October 1, 2000.

Feast Day: July 9

Patron saint of drug addicts.

Warm Up: How does this image speak to you?

Walk in Hope

ST. MARK JI TIANXIANG

We often think of righteousness as something we must enforce in others. "Who should we blame for the state of the world?" we ask ourselves. We revel in pointing out the proverbial splinter in our neighbor's eye, especially if they disagree with how we interpret justice. But that type of righteousness is only *self-righteousness.*

What if real righteousness has more to do with our own yearning to be healed? What if the hunger and thirst we experience is really the self-awareness of our own blinding "planks"? Helpless against life's traumas and unfairness, like Christ dying on the Cross we gasp, "I thirst."

St. Mark Ji Tianxiang understood this unquenchable pain. He grew up in a Catholic Christian family in China and became a doctor. He was known for his charity, often treating the poor at no cost. And then in his thirties, after taking opium to treat a stomach ailment, he became an addict. In the late nineteenth century, nothing was known about addiction, and it was believed to be simply a moral failing. We can imagine how his community must have redefined him in light of his opium use. He sought the Sacrament of Reconciliation over and over in the hope of relief, but his physical torture endured. Eventually, his priest refused to hear his Confession or administer the Eucharist to him, believing he was simply an unrepentant sinner. It was an unjust life sentence bestowed on a healer who hungered for his own healing.

Even today, addiction can still trigger a sense of shame in both patient and family. It affects every aspect of one's life—from relationships to finances to health. There are many things one can become addicted to, but the pattern starts innocently enough by a soul simply wanting relief from pain. Unfortunately, the temporary comfort quickly turns into a deadly parasite, mercilessly eroding both body and soul.

St. Mark Ji Tianxiang had none of the modern recovery treatments available today. Denied the sacraments, he could have lost faith. Instead, he held on to God as his only lifeline. He remembered who he had been: a beloved man and charitable doctor. He had hope that Christ would not forsake him. Even in his darkest times he continued to attend church, praying for salvation. Unable to attain relief from his addiction in this life, he prayed to die as a martyr, believing that giving his last breath of life for Christ might ensure his entrance to heaven.

Like Jesus, he suffered rejection from the religious establishment. Like Jesus, he was targeted by political militants— those in the Boxer Rebellion who sought to kill Christians and missionaries. Mark and his family were captured for execution, and like Jesus, he chose personal sacrifice over victimhood. He begged the executioners to kill him last so that none of his family members would have to die alone. His last act of mercy was to protect them from that injustice. He chanted the Litany of the Blessed Virgin Mary as he was beheaded.

Blessed Are They Who Hunger and Thirst for Righteousness

Why didn't Jesus heal him in his lifetime? Maybe because his faith was strong without physical healing. Maybe there was eternal purpose in his long suffering. Maybe the meaning of his life was to compassionately bring others to healing from heaven. He was a doctor, after all.

Write your Thoughts:

Prepare to Climb

A VISIO MOMENT

Turn to page forty-nine, and reflect upon this mountain image. In this painting, the figure is holding up his empty cup, hoping for a drop or two of mercy to fall from the surrounding darkness. He "wears" the mountain as an all-encasing heavy garment. Within the mountain form, within himself, is his smaller, inner child. The child also holds a vessel, but a large, empty one with only a broken heart in it.

In what ways might your own brokenness keep you enslaved in darkness? What can you ask Jesus to heal in your own soul?

JOURNAL / CHALLENGE

Think about issues of injustice that set off the biggest emo-tional response in you. Why do those causes capture your attention? Are they closely tied to your self-image or your self-worth? Ask God to help you discern what your appro-priate response should be.

It is inevitable that at times we will be misunderstood, our words or actions will be taken out of context, or we will come in contact with those who disagree with us. In "cancel culture" this can mean being dismissed or cut off entirely from a desired community. How might you practice seeing others through God's eyes and not just through your own judgments? What are ways in which you can deflect a can-cel-culture mentality within your circles of influence?

Reflect on how it must have felt for St. Mark to be rejected from receiving the sacraments of Eucharist and Reconcilia-tion because of his addiction. Have you had times in your own life when you felt rejected by your community for some-thing you could not control? Or have you ever condemned someone or a certain "type" of person without knowing or trying to understand all of the circumstances? Write or draw about your feelings around the event.

TODAY'S SMALL STEP

Are there ways that you numb pain or are unwilling to forgive yourself? Write a prayer to Jesus for help, and recite it every day. Pray for those dealing with addiction and for those in recovery.

This Is My Story

My Prayer Today

Give us this day our daily bread.

Dear Jesus:

When I am tempted to only see my faults and failings, remind me that I am made by you and sustained by you. You knew me and loved me before I was born. Keep me in gratitude, not bitterness, in all circumstances and let me lean on you, not my own understanding, in uncertain times. Help me to rely on you, Jesus, one moment at a time and not worry about yesterday or tomorrow. St. Mark Ji Tianxiang, pray for me. *Amen.*

Blessed Are the Merciful

ST. MARIA GORETTI

Go & Learn the meaning of the Words "I desire Mercy, not Sacrifice." I Did not come to call the righteous but Sinners.

Matthew 9:13

A Scripture Reading

Therefore, if you bring your gift to the altar, and there recall that your brother has anything against you, leave your gift there at the altar, go first and be reconciled with your brother, and then come and offer your gift. Settle with your opponent quickly while on the way to court with him. Otherwise your opponent will hand you over to the judge, and the judge will hand you over to the guard, and you will be thrown into prison. Amen, I say to you, you will not be released until you have paid the last penny.

—Matthew 5:23–26

"Blessed are the merciful, for they will be shown mercy."

St. Maria Goretti

Born October 16, 1890, in Marche, Italy.
Died July 6, 1902, age eleven.

Beatified April 27, 1947.
Canonized June 24, 1950.

Feast Day: July 6

Patron saint of victims of rape, crime victims, teen girls, modern youth.

Warm Up: *How does this image speak to you?*

Leave No One Behind

ST. MARIA GORETTI

Eleven-year-old Maria Goretti was viciously attacked and stabbed by an angry young man whose sexual advances she had resisted. Hours later, she died of her painful wounds. For this reason, we might be tempted to celebrate her as a tragic heroine who thwarted a rape. And yet, that is too simple a story. For this young woman embodied the very love of God, whose love goes far beyond what is reasonable or rational.

You see, even in the midst of pain and impending death, Maria insisted that her attacker be unconditionally forgiven. She prayed with her family, begging that they also extend forgiveness. That kind of response can be hard to fathom in our era of #MeToo and senseless shootings. Why would she have insisted on forgiveness with her last breath?

It might be because she was familiar with her assailant's story. Like many sexual assault victims, she knew her attacker. Her family had moved in with the Serenellis after the death of her father, when Maria was only nine years old. Alessandro would have been about seventeen. In the years they lived together, he may have spoken about his own mother's mental illness and death. Maria may have learned of his brother's suicide and his father's alcoholism. She may have seen that he suffered the emotional violence that comes from broken families. While none of this justifies his actions, it does set the scene for why he might become so obsessed with possessing and overpowering a girl who showed him everyday kindness.

All survivors of sexual assault have a primary need to be safe, and for their attackers to be held accountable. We do not remember Maria because she let go of these important needs—if she had been able to keep her agency, she likely would have sought safety and accountability. We remember her because she never let go of her fundamental dignity, even as Alessandro tried to steal that dignity from her.

Maria held such deep reverence for human dignity—her own as well as Alessandro's—that in the few final, painful moments of her life, she chose to remain free. Perhaps if she had more time, she would have been able to more fully process the suffering that Alessandro imposed on her, but as her life ebbed away by the minute, the best thing she could reach for was forgiveness. Alessandro would have to face the truth of what he had done—in his own conscience or in a court of law—but that was a process beyond her control. The one thing she *could* control was her own freedom, and by forgiving Alessandro, she refused to let his actions or her own vengeance define who she was.

God redeems everything, even bad things, for his good purpose. Mercy allows us to participate in God's creative work—Maria's forgiveness opened a door for Alessandro and brought peace to the two families.

Alessandro was convicted of his crime and spent twenty-seven years in prison. While in confinement, he became more anxious and distraught over what he had done.

One night, a smiling Maria appeared in his cell, extending to him fourteen lilies of forgiveness. He was changed in that moment, and he began to live for holiness. When he was released, he became a lay Franciscan brother working in the monastery garden. Later, he humbly asked and was granted forgiveness by Maria's mother and the local community. He was even present with the family at her canonization ceremony.

St. Maria Goretti's last words as she died were: "I forgive Alessandro and I want him with me in heaven forever."

Write your Thoughts:

Prepare to Climb

A VISIO MOMENT

Turn to page sixty-five and reflect on this mountain image. In the painting, the figure holds an olive branch, a biblical symbol of peace and harmony. She offers it forward, and it radiates an energetic, colorful light. However, she is only able to transfer this power because she has been the recipient of the same mercy from the heart of Jesus. Mercy flows throughout God's kingdom like a river, bringing life to every living thing. God will never withhold mercy; it only gets blocked by our choices, by sin against the Holy Spirit.

Where have you received mercy in your story?

JOURNAL / CHALLENGE

Have you been harmed by someone you struggle to forgive? What do you need for safety and accountability in this situation? How can you move toward freedom and healing?

Do you have something in your past that you feel is unforgivable, even after you've received the Sacrament of Reconciliation? Sometimes we allow pride to tell us that we are unworthy of forgiveness. Talk to Jesus about the power of the Holy Spirit and God's desire for you to accept his mercy. Sometimes we struggle to accept forgiveness for ourselves.

It is part of the human condition that sometimes we see the "right" thing only after doing the wrong thing. Where have you seen those contrasts in your life? How have your mistakes taken you along a path that helped you to understand God's truth? Have you learned from your mistakes, or do you continue to fall into the same emotional and behavioral traps?

Maria didn't see God's love as transactional, as an "eye for an eye." She understood that Jesus's plea for us to forgive "seven times seventy" times is key to our spending eternity in his light.

Have you held back forgiveness? Does Maria's story cause you to reconsider your choice?

TODAY'S SMALL STEP

Think about someone you know (or know about) who you feel has committed a mortal sin. Imagine the steps of brokenness their lives must hold for them to have reached such a pitiable state. Imagine how God sees them—acting toward them only in love. Now imagine that this person in this pitiable state is you. Listen as God speaks to you about how he desires for you to return to him. How would you respond?

How is God speaking to you with his love? Write a letter from God to you with your ideas.

This Is My Story

My Prayer Today

Forgive us our trespasses.

Dear Jesus:

Help me to forgive and heal. When others cause me pain, help me remember that I am your beloved. When I struggle to forgive myself, remind me of your endless mercy. Your Holy Spirit is more powerful than my pain and any apparent benefit from vengeance. It is more powerful than sin and despair. Help me lay down my burdens and walk freely toward your embrace, where you wait for me with your Sacred Heart of compassion. St. Maria Goretti, pray for me. *Amen.*

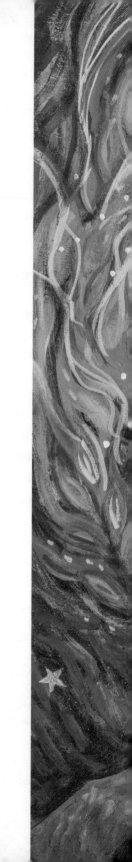

Blessed Are the Clean of Heart

ST. CHARBEL MAKHLOUF

BUT WHEN YOU PRAY GO TO YOUR Inner Room, close the door and PRAY to your Father in Secret and your Father who Sees in Secret will repay You.

Matthew 6:6

A Scripture Reading

If anyone thinks he is religious and does not bridle his tongue but deceives his heart, his religion is in vain. Religion that is pure and undefiled before God and the Father is this: to care for orphans and widows in their affliction and to keep oneself unstained by the world.

— *James 1:26–27*

Saint Charbel Makhlouf

> *"Blessed are the clean of heart,*
> *for they shall see God."*

St. Charbel Makhlouf
(Youssef Antoun Makhlouf)

Born May 8, 1828, in Bekaa Kafra, Lebanon.
Died December 24, 1898, age seventy.

Beatified December 5, 1965.
Canonized October 9, 1977.

Feast Day: July 24

Patron saint of those who suffer in body and soul.

Warm Up: How does this image speak to you?

Be the Light

ST. CHARBEL MAKHLOUF

Who would you be if you weren't burdened by distractions? No bills to pay, no sickness to worry about, no violent TV blaring through your home? Would you be kinder? Would you notice more miracles? Would you be happier?

Growing up among the cedars of Northern Lebanon, St. Charbel Makhlouf was drawn to prayerful stillness. As a child he often brought the herd of cattle he was tending to a grotto where he could pray to the Blessed Virgin Mary. His desire for deliberate retreat eventually led him to live as a hermit at St. Maron's Monastery, worshipping and praying to God for the deliverance of the world.

Taking his name, "Charbel," from a second-century martyr of Antioch venerated by both Roman Catholics and Eastern Orthodox, this Maronite monk and priest lived his life focused entirely on Christ. It is said that he never even let anyone see his face, looking up only to see heaven and the tabernacle. While his ascetic lifestyle might seem extreme, it illustrates the fruit of a heart attuned to prayer.

From the outside, St. Charbel's life might seem lonely and uneventful. And yet he was deeply immersed in the river of quantum entanglement between Creator and creature. In silence he advocated for souls against the destructive patterns of darkness, including ongoing conflicts between his Christian and Muslim countrymen. He wrote of Satan's attacks on the family as key to his evil designs against God, warning, "Preserve the warmth of the family, because the warmth of the whole world cannot make up for it."

St. Charbel understood that we must fight, not against one another, but united against the threats of evil. His mission was to pray against that darkness on behalf of others. It required a clean heart; darkness cannot drive out darkness. St. Charbel taught, "Holiness is a state of constant transformation from matter into light."

The significance of his words became clear after his death on Christmas Eve of 1898, when a fellow monk reported seeing a light emanating from the tabernacle, surrounding St. Charbel's body, and returning to the tabernacle. Many others later reported light emanating from his tomb, and thousands of healings of both body and soul have been recorded at his gravesite at the monastery. In the forty years that followed, he was exhumed multiple times and his body was found to be uncorrupted, flexible, and exuding blood and water. St. Charbel's life of constant prayer had purified his heart, making him an unhindered conduit of miraculous healings from heaven.

When we first learn to pray, we spend much of the time asking God for wishes or conveniences. As our practice deepens, we learn to talk less and listen more. We become better at discerning darkness from light, and God waits for us in the quiet, ready to reveal himself. Through prayer we find our way back to the place where the "peace . . . that surpasses all understanding" resides (Phil 4:7). There, in God, we are renewed again. We reflect his light.

We may not be called to the cloistered life like St. Charbel, but we can make a regular practice of prayer and stillness. We can pray against the forces of darkness and be a light to the world. We can look for the good in others as our brothers and sisters in the mystical Body of Christ. When we see God in others, we see the face of God.

Write your Thoughts:

Prepare to Climb

A VISIO MOMENT

Turn to page eighty-one, and reflect on this mountain image. In this painting, the figure stands on top of the mountain, on top of the large boulders, and sings praise while immersed in God's light. Judgment and darkness are gone. All colors, darks and lights, resolve into pure white light, which is seen with a clean heart.

What do you imagine it will be like to stand before God? Will your heart sing out like the figure in this artwork, or will it hide in its own shadows?

JOURNAL / CHALLENGE

Christian prayer is not a matter of tossing out words in superstitious hope or emptying our minds to nothingness. It is about listening, tuning into God's will, and letting go of unholy attachments. Where do you hold on to your own desires when talking with God? What underlying fear drives those desires? Talk to Jesus about it.

Small children have a clean heart. They play for the joy of play and are not concerned about the world outside the present moment. How can you work through childhood traumas and patterns that now distract you from having a pure heart?

A hermit physically removes all outside distraction from his life. While that might be impossible for most of us, we can each plan to devote more time to converse with God. What practices do you currently have that bring you closer to God? How can you prioritize quiet and prayer in your life?

TODAY'S SMALL STEP

Receive the Sacrament of Reconciliation and confess anything that is holding you from stepping into God's radiant light. Receive Holy Communion as often as you can for healing and nourishment as you walk toward a new state of being.

This Is My Story

ARISE TO BLESSEDNESS

My Prayer Today

As we forgive those who trespass against us.

Dear Jesus:

Open my eyes to see that when I judge others, I am often judging myself and my own fears of inadequacy. Help me let go of my own perspective, that I might hear only your voice and see only with your pure heart. Lift me above my own understanding, and give me compassion for all beings who are trying, struggling, and hurting on their way back to you. Speak to me in my darkness and show me the light of your face. St. Charbel Makhlouf, pray for me. *Amen.*

Blessed Are the Peacemakers

ST. ÓSCAR ROMERO

And the FRUIT of Righteousness is shown in PEACE for those who Cultivate Peace

James 3:18

A Scripture Reading

But I say to you, love your enemies, and pray for those who persecute you, that you may be children of your heavenly Father, for he makes this sun rise on the bad and the good, and causes rain to fall on the just and the unjust. . . . So be perfect, just as your heavenly Father is perfect.

—Matthew 5:44–45, 48

St Oscar Romero

J. NORTON

"Blessed are the peacemakers, for they will be called children of God."

St. Óscar Romero
(Óscar Arnulfo Romero y Galdámez)

Born August 15, 1917, in San Miguel, El Salvador.
Died March 24, 1980, age sixty-two.

Beatified May 23, 2015.
Canonized October 14, 2018.

Feast Day: March 24

Patron saint of Christian communicators,
El Salvador, the Americas, persecuted Christians.

Warm Up: How does this image speak to you?

All Are Welcome

ST. ÓSCAR ROMERO

Brokering peace can be dangerous business. It involves finding compromise between two sides who seek their own interests, often at the expense of the other. And it involves recognizing the evil of dividing forces.

In our world of divisions and hierarchies, it's hard for us to imagine that God's love is meant for all. How can he love those who harm us? How can he value those we don't? How in the world do we love our neighbor as we love ourselves? Perhaps it begins with each of us understanding our own place, not as gods of our own destiny, but as children of the one true God. As his children, we are all brothers and sisters, not only of each other, but of Christ. He never asks for division or domination among his family. "Us versus them" isn't God's way. Self-righteousness and unconditional love do not mix.

When St. Óscar Romero was appointed archbishop in San Salvador in 1977, he was considered a "safe" choice by both Church leaders and the right-wing government. Soft-spoken, reserved, and socially conservative, he was expected to keep the Church from becoming a pawn of leftist revolutionaries while maintaining decorum with the country's military rulers. Not making waves seemed like a justifiable form of peace in a country poised for civil war.

Three days after his installation, everything changed when his Jesuit brother Fr. Rutilio Grande, an outspoken activist for the poor, was gunned down. Suddenly, the "otherness" of the poor became extremely personal. The evil consequences of compliance with a government that persecuted its citizens became apparent. The privilege of inaction was no longer an option. Confronted firsthand with state-sponsored terror, the quiet man became what he termed a "microphone for God."

Óscar Romero began to speak out against human-rights violations, to boycott government events, and to offer sermons and news of the dead and missing through his own weekly radio show. He championed the rights of the poor and implored wealthy landowners to repent and return to the Gospel. He denounced US aid to the ruling military junta and encouraged soldiers to obey the laws of God rather than kill fellow citizens. Even with his own safety under threat, he continued to speak out, saying, "I do not believe in death without resurrection. If they kill me, I will rise again in the people of El Salvador."

Óscar Romero was assassinated while celebrating Mass.

Every despot's tactic is to silence or eliminate adversaries to maintain (the illusion of) power. We can find ourselves in that role in our own personal conflicts if we aren't careful. But that kind of "win" denies God-given dignity—both our own and that of our opponents.

Divided, we fall. Peace is a long-game venture, beginning with making peace with the insecurity of our own hearts. Can we extend empathy for other perspectives and experiences, however foreign they may seem? Anything less will result in injustice. Anything less is only repressive regime rule over another. Can we ever achieve peace and goodwill for all here on earth? Powerful forces work against it, but we can take heart—just as St. Óscar Romero did—that our peaceful Savior, Jesus, has already won victory over death for us.

Write your Thoughts:

Prepare to Climb

A VISIO MOMENT

Turn to page ninety-seven and reflect on this mountain image. The lower portion of the art represents darkness and division, with roads leading away from center and unity. As we move up the mountain, light begins to permeate the darkness, coming together in harmony at the top. Those who have done the work and reached "across the aisle" to connect with the other side enjoy the warmth of the Father's light as brothers and sisters.

Where do you see yourself in this picture?

JOURNAL / CHALLENGE

St. Óscar Romero said, "There are many things that can only be seen through eyes that have cried." Is there unhealed pain or fear in your life that leads you to judge and condemn others? Reflect on your patterns of thought and how you might let go of your desire to control others to benefit yourself.

St. Paul reminds us: "For our struggle is not with flesh and blood but with the principalities, with the powers, with the world rulers of this present darkness, with the evil spirits in the heavens" (Eph 6:12). As you consider conflicts both in the world and in your own life, examine how you might move from "us versus them" to a more unified force against evil. What ideas come to mind?

In a funeral Mass for martyred priest Fr. Octavio Ortiz Luna, St. Óscar Romero said, "How well people respond when we know how to love them." Would you think or act differently if you were loved differently? Would your enemies have become different souls had they been loved well? Consider how you might love others better for the purpose of promoting peace.

TODAY'S SMALL STEP

What are we so afraid of that makes us discount another soul rather than try to understand their point of view? Take a moment to consider the point of view of someone you completely disagree with. How might their life experiences and learned beliefs drive their choices? See them as fellow children of God, and write down as many things as you can think of that illustrate how and why they are also worthy. Make a piece of art about your answers.

This Is My Story

ARISE TO BLESSEDNESS

My Prayer Today

Lead us not into temptation.

Dear Jesus:

Remind me that I am a worker here to do your will, not the god of my own life. You are the master builder and know how all things work for your good. Protect me from thinking I am more righteous than others, and reveal the ways my choices might limit the freedom of another. Remind me that you are bigger than politics, pandemics, and world events, yet personal enough to see into my heart, between marrow and bone. Keep me from things that tempt me away from peace in my own heart, in my family, and in the world. St. Óscar Romero, pray for me. *Amen.*

Blessed Are They Who Are Persecuted

ST. JOSÉ LUIS SÁNCHEZ DEL RÍO

I will Sing of Your Majesty ABOVE THE hEAVENS with The mouths of baBes & infants. YOU HAVE Established a BuLwark aGainst Your Foes to Silence Enemy and AVenGeR.

Psalm 8:2b-3

A Scripture Reading

"Let the children come to me; do not prevent them, for the kingdom of God belongs to such as these. Amen, I say to you, whoever does not accept the kingdom of God like a child will not enter it." Then he embraced them and blessed them, placing his hands on them.

—Mark 10:14–16

SAINT

JOSÉ SANCHEZ DEL RIO

VIVO CHRISTO REY

JNEATON

*"Blessed are they who are persecuted
for the sake of righteousness,
for theirs is the Kingdom of heaven."*

St. José Luis Sánchez del Río

Born March 28, 1913, in Sahuayo, Mexico.
Died February 10, 1928, age fourteen.

Beatified November 20, 2005.
Canonized October 16, 2016.

Feast Day: February 10

Patron saint of persecuted Christians, children,
adolescents, Sahuayo (Mexico).

Warm Up: *How does this image speak to you?*

Taking the High Road

ST. JOSÉ LUIS SÁNCHEZ DEL RÍO

The Eucharist is such a humble thing—to the casual observer, only a small, circular wafer. The significance of that tiny host is lost on them. But to Catholic believers, it is life itself. It is the very Body of the man who gave everything for our salvation: Jesus, Son of God and our Good Shepherd.

To some, children are too insignificant to count. And yet faith, hope, and love are passed most authentically from parent to child. Satan knows this and constantly undermines the family and the Church's relevance in society in hopes of destroying God's kingdom. In St. José Luis Sánchez del Río's time, Mexico's focus on the elimination of Church influence in favor of populist democratic governance led to severe persecution of Catholics under many anticlerical laws. President Plutarco Elías Calles declared as part of his plan, "We must enter and take possession of the consciences of the children, of the consciences of the young, because they do belong, and should belong, to the revolution."

As his disciples came to see, Christ's revolution has nothing to do with military might or political aspirations. If we think we can secure permanent peace and justice without Christ, we have been misled by lesser gods. In the time of this young saint, the faithful knew what was being withheld

ARISE TO BLESSEDNESS

under the guise of justice: the true Source of life. Young Jose witnessed firsthand what happens when government becomes the decider of will, not the protector of it. Persecution follows. We lose influence over our children and the soul of our nation.

Under Calles's rule, priests were censored, churches and Catholic schools were closed, and people were forbidden from displaying religious items in their homes. The boy who should have still been playing with friends and enjoying the innocence of childhood instead followed his older brothers to fight with the Cristeros, a popular resistance movement that sought to defend and protect the Catholic faith. His commanding officer tried to ensure the boy's safety with noncombat tasks such as serving the troops and carrying the flag. But when the general's horse was shot dead, the boy gave him his own and stayed to fight. He was captured and tortured.

St. José Luis was held in the church where he had been baptized, which had been converted into a stable and cock-fighting corral. At one point his captors offered the boy a chance to switch sides and save his life. He refused with the battle cry, *"¡Vivo Cristo Rey!"* ("Long live Christ the King!").

When he adamantly refused to renounce his faith, his captors sliced the bottoms of his feet and forced him to walk ten blocks to his grave, where he was stabbed to death. The night before his execution, his aunt was able to slip a fragment of the Blessed Sacrament into his final meal. Jesus, the Good Shepherd, nourished him, embraced him, and walked him home. He was only fourteen years old.

Write your Thoughts:

ARISE TO BLESSEDNESS

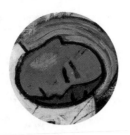

Prepare to Climb

A VISIO MOMENT

Turn to page 113, and reflect upon this mountain image. People who have survived persecution always tell stories of how God was present to them in their suffering. When others throw stones and mock us, God stands with us. His hand saves, although not always in the way we imagine.

Reflect on the stones you have thrown and the ones that have been hurled at you. Where was God in the picture? Did you know he was there?

JOURNAL ✒ CHALLENGE

At what point in your life did you first become consumed with adult concerns and perspectives? Has life convinced you to solve your problems apart from God? Have you complicated simple truths of life and death? Reflect on your answers.

When we fear judgment, we become afraid to speak up for truth, even around our own dinner tables. Lies left unchallenged become systemic. Still, Jesus stays silent and waits until we are ready to declare truth in his holy name. In what areas do you feel persecuted—even by other family members—when your defense of God's Word conflicts with others' personal beliefs?

St. José Luis never let go of his faith in Christ in the midst of evil and extreme persecution. Even as a child, he knew who Jesus was. How would you answer the question from Jesus, "But who do you say that I am?" (Mt 16:15)? Write about your response and any fears that bubble up.

TODAY'S SMALL STEP

Are you involved in local political processes, including your local school board meetings? Choose at least one way to get more involved in the schools and policies in your own area: Write a letter. Attend meetings. Donate or volunteer. Research the issues so you can make informed decisions when it comes time to vote. (Don't forget to consider who is paying for advertising and the unspoken repercussions of new laws and spending proposals.)

Do your best to vote in line with your values, and discuss your decisions with your spouse or children (as appropriate) in a respectful way.

This Is My Story

My Prayer Today

Deliver us from evil. Amen.

Dear Jesus:

Grant me the eyes to see evil coming, and help me not to fall into its empty promises of comfort and ease. When it shouts loudly, let your love speak through me at a truer frequency. Let me lean on you in my fear, and remove the veil between us. Help me to walk humbly and persevere to the end until I can be with you forever in your kingdom. St. José Luis Sánchez del Río, pray for me. *Amen.*

CONCLUSION:

Rejoice and Be Glad, for Your Reward Will Be Great

Then the Angel said to me, "Write this:

Blessed are those who have been called to the wedding feast of the Lamb. These words are true; they come from God."

Rev 19:9

A Scripture Reading

Blessed are you when they insult you and persecute you and utter every kind of evil against you [falsely] because of me. Rejoice and be glad, for your reward will be great in heaven. Thus they persecuted the prophets who were before you.

—*Matthew 5:11–12*

Reaching the Peak

When we reflect on the Stations of the Cross or the healing encounters in the Bible, we can see clearly how Jesus shows his love for us through his actions, even as he faced death. His teachings of the Beatitudes, however, are something altogether different: they call each of us to love him back.

Take a moment and imagine what that means to you now that you've had time to ponder the lives of some of our fellow blessed travelers. Is Jesus just a nice prophet from long ago with some great social-justice ideas? Or is he alive and present today, inviting you closer to him through the circumstances of your life? What does it look like for you to love him? His invitation—our calling—is accepted in living the Beatitudes. Our hope is found in their consolation that our suffering has eternal purpose. Where do you sense God is asking for your "yes"? Where are you resisting?

Hiking up a mountain is hard. On our climb up Croagh Patrick, we endured sore legs, blisters, and exhaustion. There was always threatening or unpredictable weather or the occasional injury. Even with good shoes and helpful travel companions, we still needed a bit of trust in our readiness to navigate the unknown and unexpected. As we gazed up at the far-off summit from the trailhead, we felt some trepidation for the journey ahead. In spite of that, we set off in hope of a stunning view from a new vantage point. We felt the excitement of the call.

Answering the call to a Gospel-centered life can be even more challenging. The collective world does not reward humility or weakness. When we mourn or seek righteousness, the world offers little to no compassion, preferring that we get on with it and keep producing. And it seems as if those with duplicitous hearts, those who bully, and those who create wealth from war always win.

Many saintly people, including five of the eight saints in this book, endured physical hardship and early death because of their choice to follow Christ. So why did they persist? Why might we? Because in living the Beatitudes we drive out darkness and division that might otherwise keep us from recognizing God. In choosing to give our lives away, we discover who we really are, what we were made for, and how deeply we are loved. We will hear Christ's voice clearly. We will live differently, fear less, and see the world from a higher vantage point. It is a worthy invitation to an unimaginable life. And yet . . .

And yet what sounds so reasonable in words can be desperately hard to live. It can feel as if the world is against us. Satan does not want us to be blessed or to enter heaven. He hopes you'll stay locked in your own understanding, following alternate paths away from the mountain, fraught with reminders of past sins and failed attempts at holiness. He wants you to cling to your brokenness like a badge of courage. He offers that the Beatitudes are great ideas we never have to actually live out. He wants you to be afraid and complacent—until your time runs out.

That doesn't have to happen. Chart your course with prayer, sacraments, and acts of mercy. When obstacles arise, ask Mary and the saints for guidance. As potential disciples of Jesus, each of us must answer his question at some point: "Do you also want to leave?" (Jn 6:67). Like Peter, we should hope to reply, "Master, to whom shall we go? You have the words of eternal life" (Jn 6:68).

Peter knew Jesus. He heard the words, he saw the miracles, and he felt the love firsthand. He was ready to give away everything, even his life, for a love like that. We can have a love like that too. We can know Jesus as Peter and the disciples did by doing our best to live as he taught us, trying again every day. We learn that giving away the love we've received renews our life in the Spirit. The saints in this book are just a few examples of people who understood this paradox, and we can ask them for their help in our own journey:

- In *St. André Bessette*, we see how true poverty of spirit can open us up to God's plans. Can we let go of that protective pride and let God assure us that we are good enough?

- In *St. Elizabeth Ann Seton*, we understand that mourning has purpose. Can we look to the places that bring us deep sorrow and ask God to hold us in our sorrow and return us to a deeper sense of joy?

- *St. Maximilian Kolbe* shows us that true power does not overpower. *St. Mark Ji Tianxiang* illustrates how God's timing is not limited to our earthly lives. Can we let go of our desire to control immediate outcomes and allow ourselves to be instruments of God's will?

- *St. Maria Goretti* teaches us that mercy given is mercy received, and *St. Charbel Makhlouf* shows us that through prayer God transforms darkness to his light. Can we embody a life of such generosity that those we encounter are made better for walking with us?

- Finally, *St. Óscar Romero* and *St. José Luis Sánchez del Río* illustrate why we must recognize the dignity of all people and reject any divisions of "us versus them" as false and harmful to peace. Can we rethink our comfort and possessions in light of liberty for all?

At the wedding at Cana, Jesus's mother instructed the servants to "do whatever he tells you" in order to receive the choice wine for the wedding feast (Jn 2:5). She poses the same request to us: "Will you follow my Son? Will you do what he asks? Will you trust his invitation?"

Jesus has mapped out the Way to eternal happiness with his own Body and Blood. He has taught us how to hear his voice with our hearts when our human senses deceive us. The Beatitudes challenge us beyond what we see, beyond our capabilities, beyond what we thought we knew about ourselves. They are an open invitation to peace and joy beyond our understanding. And when we arrive in heaven, at the promised wedding feast, we can sit with Jesus and lay our head upon his heart as his "favored disciple," relishing the reward of a life well-lived. We can always say no. It will be so much better if we say yes.

As you take a moment to look back over the ground you have covered in this retreat, where do you sense God is asking you to offer your "yes"?

This Is My Story

Acknowledgments

This book is dedicated to my father, the late Richard Duris. It feels strange to even write that sentence: my childhood memories of him include fear, awkwardness, and a lot of walking on proverbial eggshells. In the twenty-six years that our lives intersected, I perceived him one way. In the following three decades since his death, I have come to understand that there was more to his story, as there is for each of us.

My father was a conflicted person, and consequently so was my love for him. I witnessed him embrace a humble heart when my brother was born with Down syndrome and doctors suggested he be put in an institution (thankfully, both of my parents refused!). At other times he could be steeped in anger, enslaved by his need for order and acknowledgment. He could be loving and jovial, or self-righteous and emotionally unpredictable. He loved history and writing, yet I never saw him explore his creative side. He demanded perfection from my sisters and me, and he was quick to reprimand or shame us if we stepped out of line or caused him any undue stress. I learned to keep my feelings hidden and play the perfection game. It seemed like a good way to stay out of trouble. It's not so great for spiritual growth.

I have him to thank for my curiosity about the nature of God. My desire to understand and not be shamed has led me to seek truth. I used to believe I had to earn love, that my worthiness was in my control. I have felt the disconnect between who I want to be and what I feel on the inside. As I excavate my shadows within the events of my life, I see I possess some of the same qualities of which I once accused him. I can be dedicated and truthful, but also hypocritical and manipulating. And I know that, for both of us, those patterns were born out of a broken heart, great fear, and a need to survive. Someone taught my father to keep himself hidden and guarded too. We aren't that different.

It is in knowing his story that I can heal mine, that I can see how Jesus uses all things for his purpose. His early and difficult death transformed our relationship, empowering me and opening my heart to face future challenges differently than he did. I can see where he trusted God and where he didn't, and I have evidence of the outcome of both.

As I write these words, I am fifty-six years old, the same age he was when he passed, which has brought him to the forefront of my mind. When he died, I remember simultaneous feelings of both immense sadness and relief, freedom and guilt. In our human condition we can hold two conflicting ideals at the same time: desire for love and fear of love's vulnerability. It is the paradox we must accept to fully live the Beatitudes. To love anyway when everything in us wants to hide. To "be not afraid" when really we're terrified. Finding our way to the blessedness Jesus laid out in his first sermon can take a lifetime of seeking, and then some.

My father, me, and you are all part of a much larger mystery yet to be fully revealed. The road is both incredibly joyful and heartbreakingly painful, so we have to remember to be kind to ourselves and one another. We have to let go of perfection as a virtue worth pursuing and set aside our need for endless production and distraction. Let's walk up that mountain, sit at Jesus's feet, and listen to what he is teaching us. It's our only way to happiness.

ARISE TO BLESSEDNESS ✒ JOURNALING PAGES

ARISE TO BLESSEDNESS ✒ JOURNALING PAGES